Original title:
Tassels and Tales

Copyright © 2025 Creative Arts Management OÜ
All rights reserved.

Author: William Hawthorne
ISBN HARDBACK: 978-1-80586-116-4
ISBN PAPERBACK: 978-1-80586-588-9

Silken Echoes

In the attic there's a hat,
With ribbons that dance and flit,
Each time I wear it, oh so grand,
I trip and make the funniest wit.

A clown's nose rolls across the floor,
It seems to giggle as it leaps,
Chasing laughter, wanting more,
In this place where magic sleeps.

Feathers tickle my nose tonight,
I sneeze loud, almost take flight,
A parade of socks, mismatched too,
They waltz together, quite the view!

With flip-flops squeaking on the way,
I slip and slide, what a display!
The echoes of my playful fate,
In silly stories, I narrate.

Whirls of Fabric

In a world where garments prance,
Fabrics twirl, oh what a dance!
A sock left out, a scarf that flies,
Laughter echoes, oh my, what a surprise!

Buttons bounce in a merry chase,
While zippers giggle, keeping pace.
Stitching stories, thread unwinds,
In this fabric land, joy you find!

Chronicle of Threads

Once a thread had lots to say,
It spun a yarn in a quirky way.
With every knot, a tale unfurled,
Of silly stitches in a woolen world.

Needles poked with cheeky grins,
As fabric wrestled, chaos begins.
Spools of color blushed and laughed,
As patterns clashed in a tangled craft.

Colors that Speak

Yellow giggled, blue took a chance,
Red twirled in a vibrant dance.
Green whispered secrets, oh what fun,
While orange chuckled under the sun.

In this rainbow, hues collide,
With every shade, there's joy inside.
Patterns chattered, colors played,
In a jolly feast, laughter stayed!

Loomed Fables

In the loom where stories weave,
Waves of laughter, you won't believe!
A quirky pattern, a comic line,
Twists and turns make it divine.

A tale of a hat with no head,
Or a pair of pants that prefer to spread.
Each fable spun with a cheeky tone,
In threads of laughter, we find our home!

The Weave of Life

In a world of threads so bright,
Knots and twists bring pure delight.
Bobbins dance in joyful spree,
As we laugh at what will be.

Colors clash and patterns fight,
We stitch our dreams by day and night.
With every loop, a new surprise,
Who knew yarn could be so wise?

Strings of Connection

With every tug, a giggle grows,
Each strand held tight, that's how it goes.
We pull and stretch, but never break,
Laughter tugs at every ache.

Like tangled messes in a box,
We weave our tales, ignoring clocks.
From silly quirks to wild flair,
Our bonds are strong, beyond compare.

Intricate Journeys

In a fabric of every hue,
We wander paths, me and you.
With loops and swirls in our quest,
Every misstep brings a jest.

From the loom to the great wide space,
We stumble, but we find our place.
Each tiny stitch is a grand cheer,
For every mishap brings us near.

Unspooled Memories

With each unwind, a tale unfolds,
Moments wrapped in threads of gold.
Snippets of laughter, slips of grace,
We gather them all in our embrace.

As the spool runs low, we reminisce,
In tangled memories, we find bliss.
Though the yarn may fray and fade,
The joy we spun will never jade.

Shimmering Whispers

In the cupboard, secrets frolic,
Beads of laughter, chimes so comic.
Each thread a giggle, each knot a jest,
Bouncing ideas put humor to the test.

Dancing shadows with glimmers bright,
Twinkling stories in the soft night light.
A twirl of colors, a wink of fate,
Whispers of hilarity, never too late.

Frayed Edges

Ragged borders of tales untold,
Promises began, but never bold.
Twisted yarns with laughter stitched,
Life's own fabric, wildly pitched.

With every snag, a chuckle grows,
Fading paths where humor flows.
Frayed edges tell of clumsy friends,
Smiles sewn where the nonsense bends.

Colors of Narrative

Bright pigments splash with a cheeky grin,
Stories painted where fun begins.
A hue of giggles, a flicker of cheer,
Splashing colors, come gather near.

Brush strokes of chuckles, jests left and right,
Pinks of mischief and blues of delight.
Each tale a canvas of quirky play,
Crafted in hues that brighten the day.

Weaving the Unseen

Threads of chaos in a sneak peek,
Laughter woven, so unique.
A tapestry of whimsy laid,
Unseen wonders in antics played.

Fabric of fun, tangled but bright,
Hidden antics spark joyous flight.
Twined in the fabric, stories unfold,
Weaving hilarity, a joy to behold.

Patterns of the Past

In a cupboard full of frills,
Lies a history that spills.
A sock so bold, it talks to me,
Its partner lost, wild and free.

Old hats with feathers, a story thread,
Each stitch a laugh, where dreams are led.
Boasting colors loud and bright,
They dance in shadows, late at night.

Grandma's quilt, a patchwork cheer,
With tales of mishaps, oh so dear.
Brought to life by careless hands,
Now it sings in funny bands.

A waistcoat patched in odd designs,
With coffee stains like vintage wines.
Each rip and tear a joke to share,
In every fold, a laugh lays bare.

A Symphony in Stitch

A needle darts like lightning swift,
In fabric streets, it makes a gift.
A thread off course, what a delight,
It dances madly, left and right.

Buttons pop with giggles loud,
As patterns clash with kitsch and proud.
A patch of polka dots absurd,
A melody from each silly word.

Lace adorned with whispers sweet,
It tells of laughter, soft and neat.
A tapestry with tales askew,
Where mismatched dreams take on a view.

Knots untied in quirky spins,
Reveal the chaos where fun begins.
Socks that wed and hats that flee,
A stitched-up symphony, wild and free.

The Loom of Life

As warp and weft begin to play,
They weave the secrets of the day.
Threads of mischief, tangled neat,
Crafting patterns for our feet.

A loom spins tales of silly bliss,
Where logic bends and dreams we kiss.
Clumsy fingers twist and tease,
And every knot brings smiles with ease.

Life's a fabric, rich and bright,
With patches found in morning light.
A story spun on every side,
From rags to riches, we take pride.

A scarf that curls, a headband lost,
In laughter's clutch, we count the cost.
For in each twist, we find our way,
To revel in the laughs each day.

Twists and Turns of Yarn

A ball of yarn rolls on the floor,
It tangles up, then asks for more.
A chase ensues, we laugh and spin,
A game of cat and mouse begins.

Crochet hooks are thought to tease,
Ballet of fiber in gentle breeze.
Each loop a giggle, a quiet scream,
In every stitch, we plot and dream.

In the attic close, a whimsy found,
Skeins of color all around.
Each playful yarn a tale to weave,
In every twist, we laugh, believe.

A knitted tie that won't align,
A sweater made for a doll divine.
In every turn, a story yearns,
Life's laughter sticks, and brightly burns.

Tales of Color

In a land where socks wear stripes,
And cats can spin and juggle types,
A purple giraffe danced on a wall,
While pizza flew right over all.

Each shade would quack or giggle loud,
Frogs wore pajamas, funny and proud,
A rainbow fish baked pies in a tree,
Singing to squirrels, just to be free.

Whispered Weavings

Upon a loom of dreams and schemes,
Framed by laughter, spun into beams,
A spider knitted socks for the moon,
While raccoons danced, a silly tune.

With threads of joy and twists of fate,
They made a dress for a dancing plate,
The spoons held hands and twirled in bliss,
While forks rolled by, not wanting to miss.

Chasing Shadows in Threads

A shadow ran with wooden shoes,
Chasing bright dreams on a colorful cruise,
Where socks spilled secrets on the floor,
And hats played tag with the cupboard door.

The whispers danced with glee in the air,
As mismatched buttons spun without a care,
They laughed at the sun, who tried to catch,
Only to trip, what a splendid match!

Crafted Chronicles

In the realm of stories stitched with cheer,
A book of giggles was waiting near,
Where crayons jived and erasers flipped,
And timid pencils often slipped.

The pages turned with brilliant hues,
As rubber bands sang the silliest blues,
In every corner, a treasure trove,
Of quirky wonders and tales to wove.

Hidden Stitches in the Soul

In a closet, garments hide,
A mismatched sock, they confide.
Secrets sewn in threads so bright,
Giggles echo in the night.

Lace and buttons dance about,
Each one whispers, without doubt.
Quilts of stories stitched with care,
Patchwork dreams, beyond compare.

Yet a thimble's got a scheme,
Caught in fabric, lost in dream.
Pants that never quite align,
Who knew chaos could be fine?

Every wrinkle tells a joke,
As the old seams start to poke.
Unraveled tales twirl and spin,
Warped by laughter, bound within.

Whims of Wool and Wonder

A ball of yarn rolls down the street,
Chasing shadows, oh what a feat!
Cats lie in wait, whiskers twitch,
Pranking folks, just like a witch.

Knitted hats that look awry,
A fashion statement, oh my, my!
With every stitch, a chuckle grows,
It becomes a style nobody knows.

Frogging patterns, that's our game,
Ripping back? It's not a shame.
Every twist, a tale of fun,
Woolly wonders never done.

The needles click, a sly ballet,
Stitches leap, and knitters play.
Riddles spun from strings so bright,
Laughter weaves through every night.

Untangling the Narrative

A tangled heap of colors lies,
Yarn ball dreams, and curious sighs.
Hooking tales, both fierce and bold,
A web unfolds with laughs untold.

Knots that whisper secrets true,
Each unravel, a clue for you.
Woolen whispers, sly and sweet,
Stories hidden in the beat.

Purls that twist and turns that lean,
Patterns lurk like sights unseen.
With every tug, a giggle slips,
Oh, the fun with yarny trips!

Bright ideas dance and swirl,
In every stitch, a flag unfurl.
Crafty chaos brings delight,
As narratives twist, oh what a sight!

Woven Whimsies of the Mind

Fabric thoughts drift in light air,
Wonders woven with love and care.
Patches of dreams, a colorful quilt,
Each one giggles at the guilt.

Jumbled threads talk of the day,
In a sunny spot, they laugh and play.
Fluffy thoughts of clouds in sight,
Woolly whispers, pure delight.

Crazy patterns, a merry chase,
Swirling tales that make no space.
Crochet hooks that dance and wave,
In this yarn, we'll misbehave.

Every stitch, a twist of fate,
With whimsy woven, oh so great!
Smirking buttons watch the show,
As creativity starts to flow.

Beyond the Stitch

In a cluttered shop with colors so bright,
A sock once got lost in a whimsical fight.
With buttons and yarn, it fought day and night,
'Til it tickled a cat, what a marvelous sight!

Laces were tangled, and so was the thread,
A scarf teased a mitten - 'You'd look great in red!'
They danced on the counter, quite full of dread,
For soon they would end up in boxes instead.

A quilt had a secret, a pocket of dreams,
Filled with odd buttons and glittery beams.
It whispered in twilight, or so it seems,
About how it tangled up with moonbeams.

So let's raise a glass to the threads in the air,
To the prancing of garments, a fanciful flare.
For in all the stitches, there's laughter to share,
In the silly capers of fabric laid bare.

Echoes of the Loom

In the corner, a yarn ball rolled down the way,
It giggled and bounced, what a playful display.
Next to it sat a needle, sharp as a ray,
Who swore she could stitch the whole world by May.

A fabric forgot how to stay in a line,
It looped and it swirled, making patterns divine.
It twirled with a bow, oh so twisty and fine,
Until it got dizzy and needed some wine.

A tale of old sweaters that lost their soft charm,
They plotted in whispers to cause quite the harm.
But when they got out, they only spread calm,
Drawing laughter from everyone with their yarny disarm.

So gather your spools and your colorful thread,
For weaving together is just what we need.
Let's stitch up some joy and not worry or dread,
In this tapestry of giggles, our heart shall be fed.

Threads of the Forgotten

A coat in the corner, forgotten by years,
Whispers of laughter mixed with some tears.
It dreamed of adventures, wild 'round the peers,
Yet now it just hangs, collecting dust spheres.

Old patches and seams have stories to tell,
Of dances and picnics, and mischief as well.
But time has a way of casting a spell,
Leaving ghosts of those moments in fabric's own shell.

A pocket too small held secrets so grand,
Of gumdrops and treasures tucked carefully planned.
Yet now it just sighs, with no childish hand,
To share all the wonders of being so spanned.

Let's lift up the pieces, make magic anew,
With laughter to brighten each colorful hue.
For in every stitch, there's a tale overdue,
Of joy sewn together and friendships so true.

Crafted Connections

Two gloves on a shelf looked so lonely and blue,
They stretched and they sighed, wishing for two.
They dreamed of a hand that would slip in, it's true,
To dance in the snow, with laughter anew.

The fabric of friendship is woven so tight,
With threads that are merry, oh what a delight!
They giggled and chirped through each day and night,
Crafting joy in the moments, hearts feeling quite light.

A patchwork of memories sewn by delight,
Of picnic adventures beneath stars so bright.
They stitched up their woes until dawn took its flight,
In this joyful embrace, spirits soaring in height.

So gather your scraps, let your laughter combine,
For each little piece has a story to shine.
Together with whimsy, let your heart intertwine,
In a crazy creation that's naturally fine.

Echoes in Embroidery

In a world of thread and spark,
Wobbly stitches make their mark.
A cat jumped in, the scene was set,
Now my quilt's a fuzzy pet.

Granny's tales in fabric spun,
Each patch a laugh, a joke, a pun.
A dragon stitched with crooked flair,
Looks more like fish with floppy hair.

Needles darting, colors clash,
My apron's now a vibrant sash.
An elephant in pink and blue,
Squeaks when I step—who knew?

So here's to mishaps and delight,
In every seam our quirks ignite.
We'll dance through fabric, laugh and play,
Crafty smiles chase blues away.

Stories in Stitches

Once I sewed a hat so grand,
It slipped right off; my face turned bland.
A clown appeared, oh what a shock,
And now my head's a running joke!

In patches bright, my life unfolds,
Each thread a tale that rarely holds.
A rabbit hops, a turtle crawls,
It's hard to keep track; they've made their calls.

Unruly threads and tangled yarn,
In my closet, there's a barn!
A cow that moos in colors rare,
Stitched to my socks, don't you dare!

From laughter flows a quirky bliss,
With every stitch, we wink and twist.
In this fabric fun, we weave our tales,
And lose ourselves in joking flails.

Looms of the Past

In dusty rooms where secrets hide,
Old looms whisper tales side by side.
A ghostly weaver, face aglow,
Once stitched a sweater—look at it grow!

Threads from grandpa, colors wild,
He claimed it made him feel like a child.
A vest went missing, found on a chair,
Turns out it's now the cat's new lair!

Tangled yarn from bygone days,
A slinky skirt in comical ways.
As needles prance and bobbins spin,
The ghosts of laughter boldly grin.

So here we twirl in silly flair,
Wearing remnants of yesteryear's dare.
In every knot, there's humor spun,
A time machine where laughs outrun.

The Fabric of Whimsy

A patchwork purse, oh what a sight,
Holds knickknacks that dance at night.
Buttons bouncing, giggling loud,
This purse alone could charm a crowd.

With every stitch, the stories blend,
Of socks that vanished, socks that bend.
A patch with penguins in a race,
I wear it proud—no shame, no grace!

When fabric talks and buttons sing,
It weaves a joy that makes us swing.
A magical world of snips and seams,
Where laughter reigns and dreams are themes.

So join me in this clumsy thread,
Where whimsy lives and puns are bred.
We'll wrap ourselves in goofy cheer,
In every seam, the fun is clear!

Looming Possibilities

In the corner, a loom creaks soft,
Threads dancing like they're aloft.
A cat stretches, a yarn ball flies,
What a sight, oh how time flies!

Colorful chaos in every stitch,
A rogue thread playfully starts to glitch.
Grandma laughs, with mischief's cheer,
"Oops! Looks like we've got a new idea here!"

Fabric scheming, a plot so bold,
A patchwork tale just waiting to unfold.
With every twist, new laughter spins,
Who knew that weaving could lead to grins?

As patterns twist and stories run,
Life's a fabric sewn, oh what fun!
Each knot a giggle, every loop a surprise,
In this world of stitches, joy never dies!

Fabrications of Freedom

In the room where colors collide,
A wild adventure we cannot hide.
Strings of humor drift through the air,
As mismatched socks spark a daring dare!

Once a simple thread, now a kite,
Soaring through an imaginative flight.
Unruly frays wave like flags,
Creating a circus of playful jags!

Buttons bounce and fabrics sway,
Each a character in this lively play.
Dancing squirrels, a patchwork crew,
In this craft, freedom takes a cue!

So pick up your needle, join the fun,
Stitching laughter till the day is done.
Each knot a giggle, every seam a jest,
In this playful realm, we are all blessed!

Narratives in Fiber

We weave tales with threads of delight,
Snippets of laughter fill the night.
A parrot in a shawl, what a sight!
Spinning stories, we take flight!

Each stitch a word, each knot a rhyme,
In this fabric world, we beat time.
Silly patterns, a plaid so bold,
Who knew yarn had stories untold!

Puppies weave dreams in tangled yarn,
While hedgehogs play in the yard of charm.
An owl hoots wisdom from the fringe,
Chasing worries as we all cringe!

Crafting joy, one thread at a time,
In fibers we find our silly mime.
Each loop a laugh, a chuckle spun,
In this narrative, we're all young!

Chronicles of the Woven

In the land where fibers frolic free,
A jester weaves with glee, oh me!
Colors clash and patterns play,
Every stitch a laugh, night or day!

A quilt made of giggles and snickers,
Bouncing back with warm glimmers.
Sashes dance, poking fun,
As yarn chases the golden sun!

Tales of thread shenanigans soar,
A tapestry of laughter, never a bore.
Each loop a quirk, each weave a jest,
In this fabric world, we're all blessed!

So grab your needles, let's create,
A chronicle woven, oh, it's great!
Together we spin, with stitches so bright,
In the world of threads, we find our light!

The Continuum of Fabricated Dreams

In a world where fibers twist,
A cat wore my hat, just to enlist.
With colors that clash and designs that daze,
Unraveled laughs in a fabric maze.

A sock puppet chorus takes the stage,
Spinning tall tales, full of rage.
My grandma's quilt tells stories bold,
Of dragons and knights, and potions of gold.

Each thread a joke, each stitch a pun,
In this patchwork life, we have our fun.
As fabric falls apart with grace,
It stitches up joy in every space.

So grab a needle, thread your whims,
Let's patch up fate with borrowed hymns.
We'll sew our laughter into the seams,
In this continuum of wild dreams.

Textures of Time and Truth

In pockets of fabric, secrets rest,
A collar that squeaks on a chubby chest.
Buttons that giggle find their place,
As zippers confess with a wild face.

Measured by stitches, stories leap,
From looms of laughter, we no longer keep.
As yarn spins yarn, and ribbons recount,
The zany adventures that life's about.

A scarf once worn by a cheeky crow,
Tells tales of mischief wherever winds blow.
Cuffs that rumble beneath the sun,
Blame it all on a fabric run.

With textures of laughs stitched in every guise,
Life's fabric unfolds in a twinkle of eyes.
So let's twirl in our garments, with glee and grace,
In this comedy quilt, we find our place.

Fringed Dreams

Frayed edges dance in the summer air,
While socks argue over who should care.
With fringes flapping, they take a chance,
To weave a story in a silly dance.

A vest from the '80s with polka dots,
Claims to know where the laughter's caught.
It jives to music only it can hear,
Flashing vintage secrets, oh so dear!

As patches and patterns collide in cheer,
Fringed dreams whisper what we hold near.
Each slice of fabric, a tickle and tease,
Sewing up smiles like a gentle breeze.

So let's flaunt our styles without any shame,
In this world of fabric, we all play the game.
With fringes and giggles, together we beam,
In a tapestry woven of cheerful dreams.

Whispers of Threads

Threads that chatter in the night,
Spin tales of cats and their delight.
Each yarn unravels a funny quip,
In the laughter-laden fabric strip.

A costume for mischief with sequins bright,
Hides a treasure of giggles in plain sight.
With hats that dance on a doggone whim,
We wrap our gaffes in a frolicsome hymn.

In weaving workshops, where stories unfold,
A mop dressed as a hero becomes quite bold.
Draped in humor, with every thread,
The stitches of folly are joyously spread.

So gather your remnants, and stitch up with care,
In a quilt of laughter, we have room to spare.
As threads share laughter, from old to new,
Each whisper we craft brings a chuckle or two.

Stitched Stories of Old

In a closet full of fluff,
Lie stories stitched with love.
Each thread a giggle, a snort,
Of things too wild to report.

A button here, a patch of glee,
The fabric knows, oh yes, it's me.
Whimsical tales sewn neat and tight,
In a quilt that dances in moonlight.

A thread unravels, we laugh and shout,
Did cat or dog make this one sprout?
A tapestry of chuckles spun,
As daylight fades, the fun's begun.

So gather round, my dears, come see,
The memories wrapped in mystery.
Each stitch a giggle, every fold,
A patchwork saga waiting to be told.

Adornments of the Heart

Bangles jingle with delight,
As we twirl and shimmy, light.
A necklace of jokes, we wear with pride,
In our laughter, we cannot hide.

Rings of mischief, shiny bright,
Some are big, some fit just right.
Each charm a promise, silly yet true,
A heart so full, it bursts right through.

Scarves that flutter, dance in the breeze,
Whispering secrets just like leaves.
With every twirl, a giggling sigh,
For adornments bring us joy, oh my!

So wear your quirks and don your flair,
With a chuckle, shake your hair.
In our hearts, the treasures lie,
As we frolic beneath the sky.

Layers of Time and Texture

Under layers, whispers creep,
In vintage finds, our treasures sleep.
A frock with stories, a laugh or two,
Each wrinkle tells what we once knew.

Beneath the fabric, tales unwind,
Oh, the joy we seek to find!
A hat that once made someone grin,
When adventures began within.

Frayed edges hold the best of fun,
A patchwork life we've all begun.
With every fold, we share a laugh,
As memories dance, a lively craft.

So let's unravel these threads of gold,
With every layer, let's be bold.
For under the stitches, every hue,
Lies the joy that once was you.

The Weaving of Secrets

In the loom where giggles grow,
Secrets weave, in ebb and flow.
Each strand a whisper, a sly little tease,
Binding laughter with graceful ease.

The fabric vibrates with delight,
As stories mingle, day and night.
A tapestry of cheeky grins,
Where each new tale of whim begins.

Threads intertwine, a dance sublime,
In patterns lost to passing time.
Woven into each twist and spin,
A joyous life, where fun can begin.

So peer into these layers bright,
Where even shadows feel the light.
In every secret, a sparkling dream,
As the weavings create our silly theme.

Flapping Fabrics

The curtain flaps with style,
It twists and turns, oh so wild!
The breeze makes it dance and sway,
A fabric show that steals the day.

A shirt that shrieks when tugged too tight,
Socks that vanish, oh what a fright!
Pillowcases hold secrets deep,
While blankets snicker when you sleep.

The tablecloth plays peek-a-boo,
Hiding crumbs, it knows what to do.
Dish towels tumble in a row,
Laughing at where they shouldn't go.

In every fold, a joke to tell,
A story wrapped, a cotton spell.
With hysteria, it whirls around,
In this fabric world, fun is found.

Stories Woven in Yarn

In a corner, balls of fluff,
Wobbly actions, never tough.
Knitting needles dance in pairs,
Creating tales that few compares.

A scarf that tickles, long and wide,
Wrap it snug, don't let it slide!
Each stitch a giggle, tight and neat,
A cozy hug for chilly feet.

The yarn once knotted, swears it's fine,
While in the basket, it will whine.
"Unravel me, let's make a mess,
I'm tired of all this tight finesse!"

Then tangled threads laugh, "We must play!"
While grandmas doze, they flip away.
And in their frolic, secrets spin,
In every twist, we laugh and grin.

The Dance of Loose Ends

Loose ends waltzing in a heap,
Threadbare hopes, they mustn't sleep.
A ribbon here, a string or two,
They tango, joined by silly glue.

Buttons jump with glee and cheer,
While zippers hiccup, drawing near.
A belt that flops when no one's watch,
Laughing as it makes you botch.

Old scraps whisper tales of lore,
Each cut and stitch, a memory's score.
They plot mischief in the night,
While shadows giggle, hearts take flight.

With laughter bursting from each fold,
Loose ends keep secrets yet untold.
They bind together, oh so free,
In their dance, we find the glee.

Threads of Memory

Threads of color, bright and bold,
Each one weaves a tale retold.
A golden string, a silver line,
Whispers of laughter, oh so fine.

They tangle up in silly knots,
Retelling jokes like old-time spots.
A memory drops with each little pull,
As threads run wild, the heart is full.

Stitches snicker, secrets they keep,
In the closet where they leap.
A patch that trembles, full of glee,
Unfolds the past, it wants to be free.

Every fiber, a moment's trace,
In the loom, we find our place.
With every tug, we stitch the fun,
Threads of memory, we're never done.

Frayed Memories

Once a scarf of vibrant hue,
Lost its charm, now off askew.
Puppies play, they tug and pull,
What was steady, now looks full.

Grandma's quilt, now with a patch,
Every fray a story to catch.
Laughter echoes in the thread,
As we recall what Grandma said.

Buttons bouncing off the wall,
Who knew buttons could be tall?
In the chaos, giggles rise,
In our hearts, a sweet surprise.

Memories stitched with quirky cheer,
As we smile while we hold dear.
Life's a tapestry, come what may,
With every knot, we find our way.

Bound by Yarn

In a basket, colors blend,
A tangled mass, no clear end.
Cats parade, a yarn parade,
Pouncing softly, plans are laid.

Knit one, purl two, off the chart,
A scarf so silly, it won't start.
With every stitch that goes astray,
We laugh at how we lost our way.

Friends gather with needles bright,
Battling yarn in the dim light.
Whispers trade with every loop,
As laughter bounds through this strange group.

But when the work is said and done,
What was chaos is now just fun.
Tangled yarns we hold so dear,
In every twist, we share a cheer.

Knotting Secrets

In my pocket, secrets hide,
Tied in yarn, not much to bide.
A silly tale, I weave with care,
As friends all watch my tangled affair.

Knotting stories, one by one,
Each noose binds laughter, oh what fun!
With a slip and a wink, watch it fray,
Who knew yarn could lead the way?

What's a loop without a grin?
A clumsy dance that pulls us in.
Beneath the folds, a tale does live,
Every mishap, so much to give.

A curious knot beneath my shoe,
With laughter's bounce, I step right through.
In every mishap, freedom sings,
For secrets dance with playful strings.

The Art of Unraveling

With a tug, the yarn unwinds,
Laughter echoes, joy that binds.
What's a project without a flop?
Ripping seams, oh, let it drop!

A hat turned vest, oh my, oh dear,
Creative chaos brings us cheer.
In the midst of frays and slips,
We share giggles, give our quips.

When yarn trips up my steady hands,
I'm the jester in the stands.
Clumsy knots become a show,
In this circus, laughter flows.

So here's to threads that tangle tight,
Each mishap sparks a burst of light.
As we unravel, find what's real,
In every loop, we dance and feel.

Colorful Chronicles

In a town where colors dance,
A purple cat lost its chance,
To win the race against a snail,
With dreams of great, but it would fail.

When the sun decided to snooze,
The grass wore socks, blue and loose,
Birds chirped jokes, oh what a sight,
A comic show by day and night.

The baker baked a rainbow pie,
With sprinkles launched from way up high,
But when it landed on the chef,
He laughed so hard, he lost his breath.

Each hue a story, vivid and wild,
With giggles echoing, sweet and mild,
In a quirky place where laughter steams,
And every day is filled with dreams.

Stitching the Unknown

In a closet where odd socks hide,
Lived a button with too much pride,
Dreaming to be on a shirt so tight,
Alas, it wasn't quite its night.

A needle danced, oh what a sight,
Stitching stories, left and right,
But tangled threads, a comedy gold,
Left the fabric quite uncontrolled.

One patch told jokes of years gone by,
While another tried to learn to fly,
Together they giggled, quilted in cheer,
Making warm hugs for all, my dear.

In each fold, a secret tucked,
Of laughter shared and stitches plucked,
A tapestry woven with thread and jest,
Where every seam is a playful quest.

Tapestry of Whispers

In a room where whispers spun,
Lived a fairy with a funny bun,
She tickled threads with playful glee,
   Creating giggles for all to see.

A tapestry hung with tales so light,
Of a fish who dreamed to take flight,
It flopped and quacked, what an act,
Leaving all the viewers quite intact.

Buttons bounced to a funky beat,
As patterns formed beneath their feet,
   Every twist a chuckle bestowed,
In a world where silly stories flowed.

With each stitch, secrets were shared,
A riot of laughter, nothing compared,
For in the weave of life's light play,
   Every whisper has a funny way.

Textural Tales

In a land where fabrics speak,
A woolly sheep felt quite unique,
He wore a coat, a patchwork bright,
With mismatched socks, a funny sight.

A velvet frog croaked silly rhymes,
In a garden where laughter chimes,
His lily pad was lost in style,
But his croaks could make you laugh awhile.

The denim ducks were quite the crew,
In a game of hide and seek they flew,
Their laughter rang from hills to dales,
As they spun their quirky tales.

Each texture held a riddle bold,
From fuzzy to sleek, stories told,
In a world stitched with smiles galore,
Where every giggle opens a door.

Silken Stories

In a world where ribbons dance,
Threads decide their own romance.
A fumble here, a twist gone by,
Oops! That's how my waistcoat's shy.

What if the stitches told a joke?
Laughter woven, like a cloak.
A patchwork quilt with tales to spin,
Pranks that start with a thread and grin.

Buttons pop with every chuckle,
While fabrics find their rhythm, a shuffle.
With every seam and every fold,
A wise remark that's never old.

So tip your hat, and give a cheer,
For the stories fabric likes to share.
In a closet full of playful lore,
Each layer hidden, forever more.

The Fringe Beneath

Beneath the layers, frayed but bright,
A secret life, oh what a sight!
Strings that dangle, daring the bold,
Whispering tales of mischief untold.

A curtain blushes, sways in jest,
As socks form leagues on a secret quest.
One sock lost, the other remains,
Plan hatching in colorful chains.

Lace loses its dignity for fun,
When a shoefoot's battle has begun.
Each knot a giggle, each thread a roar,
Who knew fabrics could dream and explore?

So tiptoe softly, heed the hum,
The fringe below knows where it's from.
A world alive, in colors and play,
In the depths of fabric, stories sway.

Twists of Fabric

A twirl of yarn with a wink and cheer,
Spinning tales we love to hear.
A bit of plaid in a polka dot spree,
What's the fashion? A wild spree!

Knots that wiggle in a lively dance,
Calico pranks take silly chance.
Caught up in stitches, they giggle and play,
Creating chaos at the end of the day.

Fripperies flapping, making demands,
Whispering secrets with sly little hands.
The snags and bends, a mischievous sign,
Where threads waltz and dreams intertwine.

So let's unroll this fabric parade,
Where quirky humor never will fade.
Each twist and turn, a wink to befriend,
In the world of weaves, the fun never ends.

Textures of Time

In every weave, a memory bides,
Giggles trapped in fabric rides.
From quilts that tell of rainy days,
To shirts that dance in sunlit rays.

Each swatch a story waiting to burst,
Like a shirt that's still holding the thirst.
For a day of pranks and playful spree,
Where hobby and habit live so free.

Seams that part with a cheeky shout,
Cutting in line, there's no doubt.
When socks become a pair's best friend,
And silly hats make the laughter blend.

So gather round, let the fabrics unite,
For textures of time are pure delight.
Woven together in unpredictable rhyme,
In every stitch, a chuckle defies time.

Fables at the Fabric's Edge

At the seamstress's table, a cat took a nap,
Dreaming of ribbons and a fancy new cap.
With yarn in her claws, she tied a great knot,
A tale of mischief, all woven on the spot.

A parrot in feathers said, "I can sing!"
While a tailor just grumbled, "That's quite the fling!"
He slipped on a spool and went into a spin,
Now a dance with the fabric, it seems to begin!

The dog in the corner, proud of his thread,
Chased after the mice, who'd gone off to bed.
Hewled with a laugh, as they scampered away,
Leaving him tangled - what a price to pay!

Each stitch holds a story, every patch a jest,
From knots made in chaos, we fashion our best.
So here's to the fabric, where laughter takes flight,
In woven adventures, we find our delight.

In the Shadow of Beads

In shadows of beads, a gnome had a plight,
He danced with his buttons, oh, what a sight!
With his tiny green shoes, he twirled and he spun,
Making tunes out of beads, oh what silly fun!

A dragonfly buzzed, wearing glasses so round,
Said, "Watch out, dear gnome, for that snare on the ground!"
But the gnome just laughed and jumped higher with glee,
Tripped on a necklace, then fell with a spree!

Nearby a wise owl hooted, "Just look at that fowl!"
As the gnome got back up, he began to scowl.
But the beads were a treasure, a jingle, a jive,
He donned his new bling and felt super alive!

So if ever you're trapped in the humdrum of day,
Just find you some beads and let laughter play.
As the gnome gives a twirl, you'll soon hear a cheer,
With mischief and magic, let joy persevere!

The Tapestry of Heartstrings

In a quirky old shop, where the threads intertwine,
Lived a squirrel named Nutty who loved to design.
He stitched up a blanket of dreams on a whim,
And all of his neighbors came over to swim.

The fabric was lively, with colors so bright,
A penguin in pajamas joined in with delight.
They splashed among patterns, while tails waved around,
What a raucous revival, a mess to be found!

A hedgehog brought cupcakes in shapes of pure fluff,
"I've frosted your dreams, is that not enough?"
With confetti and laughter, they wove through the night,
Drafting stories of whimsy, their hearts took flight.

So gather your friends, let the laughter unfurl,
In a tapestry woven, let whimsy swirl.
With each playful stitch, new tales come to play,
In the heart of the fabric, joy finds its way.

Laces and Legends Intertwined

In a cobbler's workshop, adventures begin,
With laces and legends tied up in a spin.
A jackrabbit bounced with shoes tied so tight,
He tripped on his laces and flew into the night!

A tortoise named Timmy was rugged and spry,
He wore shoes made of leaves, oh my, oh my!
With each little shuffle, a rustle would play,
A melody formed from leaves in ballet!

The bumblebee buzzed in a boot full of honey,
Cried, "Taste my sweet fortune, it's oh so funny!"
As they danced through the shop, laughter unraveled,
Their playful antics could leave you all baffled.

So untie your doubts and lace up some cheer,
For every old legend brings fun ever near.
In the cobbler's embrace, where silliness shines,
With laces and laughter, each story aligns.

Weaving Wonders

In a village where llamas wear hats,
The weavers chat, and laughter splats.
A thread got lost in the old brown rug,
A mouse took it home, now he's a snug bug.

At the market, a spool rolled away,
It danced like a child, brightening the day.
A cat tried to pounce, but slipped on a yarn,
Now it's a legend, told with a charm.

An owl perched high, flaunting his thread,
Claiming he weaved his own comfy bed.
But the truth came out, with a giggle and grin,
His mom did the work, with her best crafty spin.

So in this quirky place, we all see with glee,
Threads tell the tales of the funny esprit.
With laughter and knots, we weave our delight,
In a world full of whimsy, both day and night.

Fibers of Imagination

In a loom shop where everything's bright,
A squirrel slipped in, looking for a bite.
He took a spool and ran full speed,
Now he's the prince of the fiber seed.

A gnome with a beard, tangled in thread,
Told tales of a bunny, who knitted in bed.
With all of his heart and some tea by his side,
He crafted a sweater for winter's cold ride.

A spider on a mission, weaving a prank,
Laced up a scarf and snagged a good rank.
He strung a soft web, but it burst in the rain,
Now he tells jokes while he dances again.

So we gather our fibers, let stories take flight,
With laughter and joy, we stay up at night.
In this playful world, imagination reigns,
As we spin and we roll, letting humor remain.

Shades of the Untold

A tale once woven in colors so bright,
A rabbit wore orange, a duck dressed in white.
With patterns that clashed, a rainbow parade,
It turned into chaos—what a color charade!

A lion who roared in a plaid-tartan suit,
Claimed he was "stylish," but that was the root.
Critters gathered around, they couldn't help laugh,
At the king of the jungle, in a plaid crafted half.

An anteater wove tales in fabric so fine,
But all his creations came out just like swine.
With stripes and with polka dots, fun tales to tell,
His sweaters became infamous, they fit oh so well.

In the shades of the untold, fun colors they mix,
Every laugh that we share, just adds to the tricks.
In this fabric of fun, old stories come round,
With hues of delight, where giggles abound.

Tangled Narratives

A hedgehog who pranced in a tangle of strings,
Claimed he was destined for marvelous things.
But tripped over yarn, with a roll and a spin,
Now he just giggles, "It's the mess that I'm in!"

A fox in a cap, with patches and flair,
Tried to impress but got caught in mid-air.
He spun in a circle, and with quite a fuss,
Ended up tangled in a dose of good luck.

A deer with a scarf made of leftover shreds,
Wove tales of the night while munching on breads.
With stories in knots and threads tying tight,
Each laugh weaves the magic, as we stay up all night.

So here we gather, in a tangled embrace,
With narratives bouncing all over the place.
In the threads of our laughter, together we'll play,
Creating a world where humor holds sway.

Knots Tied in Silence

A string in a tangle, what a sight,
The cat's had a dance, oh what a night!
With every tug, it squeaks, it groans,
A game of catch with invisible phones.

The dog strolls by, giving me a glare,
"You think that you're clever? That's just not fair!"
But the mouse on the table is plotting a scheme,
In this fabric of chaos, they all dare to dream.

Now threads in the air, flying high,
Each one a story, as they drift and fly.
The world is a circus, a very loose thread,
We laugh in the chaos, let's dance instead!

So grab your scissors, snip and cut,
Life's too short for a neatly tied rut!
With strings in our hands, we'll weave a good tale,
Laughing at knots that attempt to prevail.

Threads of Fate Unraveled

In the attic, dust motes float like dreams,
Each thread tells a joke, or so it seems.
A sock lost in time, a button with flair,
Who knew a closet could hold such despair?

The broom laughs softly, it knows all the tricks,
Of tangled rumors and misdirected licks.
With every twist and turn, we all stumble in,
'Cause life's a patchwork, of laughter and spin.

A grandmother's quilt, full of patches and tears,
Each stitch is a giggle, a few friendly sneers.
As we sit by the fire, folly in the air,
We'll weave in our whims without any care.

So come join the laughter, let's make it a spree,
For the threads of our fates are as wild as can be!
In this tapestry woven, with stories anew,
Each bobbin a tale, each color a clue.

Adrift in a Sea of Color

A palette of hues, flung far and wide,
With bright polka dots sailing the tide.
The stripes on the waves giggle and sway,
While the cherries in boats plan a wild getaway.

The orange sun winks, a jester today,
Painting the fabric of a light-hearted fray.
While bluebirds debate which hue's the best,
Their chatter a riddle, a colorful jest.

Each splash tells a story, each drop a delight,
Of pirates in rainbow ships sailing through night.
We ride on the whimsy, like kites in the breeze,
With laughter in our sails, we float with such ease.

So grab your brush, let's paint on the fun,
In this sea of color, there's room for everyone!
With giggles and splashes, we dance on the shore,
In a world full of whimsy, who could ask for more?

The Fabric of Folklore

Under the quilt of legends long spun,
Every tale weaves a giggle, every twist a pun.
There's a socks-stealing gnome, quite the character,
And a cat with a lute, what a spectacular!

The fairies in bloom are plotting a play,
With lace for their costumes, they dance and sway.
A carrot knight fumbles, but cheers fill the air,
As laughter erupts from the castle of hair!

With threads of adventure and yarns of delight,
Each stitch in the fabric ignites laughter bright.
Folklore is fun if you give it a go,
We'll weave the absurd, let our imaginations flow.

So gather 'round friends, for the stories are vast,
With whimsical wonders and echoes that last.
We'll tie up the endings with humor and song,
In the fabric of laughter, we all will belong.

Strands of Legacy

In grandma's attic, dust flies wide,
Old hats and scarves, all set aside.
A wig on a mannequin, grinning bright,
An outfit so flashy, it gives quite a fright.

A sweater with holes, a story it tells,
Of parties gone wrong and the odor of gels.
With buttons that pop, and colors that clash,
It's a fashion disaster, all ready to bash.

From ribbons to rosettes, a curious sight,
Each strand a reminder of lost fashion fights.
With laughter we ponder, those styles of yore,
Where less was not more, and charm was just poor.

Yet tangled in threads, we shrug and we smile,
Each relic a journey, each mess has its style.
In laughter, we find the joy we can keep,
As we weave through the history, a legacy deep.

Fabrics of Fate

In a quilt made with laughter, patches so bright,
Each square tells a tale, a quirky delight.
Stitched by the hands of a cat-loving queen,
Whose choice of color is seldom seen.

With stripes that clash and polka dots near,
A masterpiece woven in humor, oh dear!
At night it brings warmth, but dreams take a twist,
As ghosts of the fabric begin to insist.

"Remember the time with the socks paired askew?
You wore bright pink crocs, and that shirt of deep blue?"
We chuckle and giggle, the chaos holds sway,
In a world of mismatches, we're all here to stay.

So let's wrap ourselves in this fabric of fates,
Where laughter is stitched in! Oh, how it creates!
With every thread tangled, we dance with delight,
Making fun out of life, though it's often a fright!

Hues of History

In a painting so vivid, with colors that clash,
A royal in purple, but shoes made of trash.
His crown's upside down, and his pants are too tight,
Yet there's joy in the blending that brings such a light.

A portrait of laughter, each brushstroke a jest,
With shades of the past, our clumsy best.
The artists just giggle, with each drip and drop,
Creating a spectacle, they just cannot stop.

From greens of old foliage to yellows that scream,
Each hue tells a tale, each wrinkle a dream.
With hieroglyphs scrawled, and patterns so wild,
History's whimsy is just that—unfiled!

So gaze upon hues that twist time and space,
Where joy is the canvas and smiles fill the place.
In laughter we linger, as colors engage,
Each moments a brushstroke, a turn of the page.

Knotted Journeys

With shoelaces tangled, and yarn left astray,
We trip through our journeys in a hilarious way.
Each knot tells a story, each twist makes us grin,
As we fumble and tumble, our laughter begins.

In a maze of missteps, a journey we share,
With socks that do vanish, causing quite a scare.
A hat on a raccoon, stealing the show,
Wearing misfortune just like a bow.

With laces and strings, the world plays its game,
Each snarl a reminder of life—and its fame.
We tiptoe on paths where the goofy delight,
Finding joy in the chaos, wrapped up tight.

So here's to our journeys, all knotted and tied,
With laughter our compass, and humor our guide.
Let's wander together, where absurdity reigns,
In the knots of our stories, the fun never wanes.

Fringes of the Unknown

In a closet hung a strange thread,
Mysterious patterns, but less than well bred.
A sock claimed it spoke with a giggle and sway,
'Look at me dance, in a silly ballet!'

The dog thought it was a snack that might bite,
He wagged and he woofed, ready for a fight.
But the thread just unraveled, fell down with a laugh,
'Today, I'm a scarf! Care for a photograph?'

The cat on the shelf, rolled her eyes with a grin,
'You think you're so fancy? You're just made of tin!'
Yet the thread swirled around, a most curious sight,
Brought everybody joy on that whimsical night.

So remember dear friends, what hangs in your space,
Might have stories to tell or a colorful grace.
In the box of old odds, in the fringe of your style,
Lies laughter and fun, wrapped in fabric for a while.

Woven Echoes

Once a yarn ball rolled off on its spree,
Bounced past a gopher, who shouted with glee.
'Where you off to, o thread, so bold?'
'Chasing the stories that never grow old!'

Through gardens it tumbled, past flowers in play,
Telling the daisies of adventures all day.
'Oh, can you believe I met a sock with a hat?'
'Don't you mean sock puppet?' said Grandma Cat.

They snickered and chuckled, swapping their lore,
While the purple thread danced, couldn't help but explore.
Echoing laughter like a bright sunny tune,
Creating a mishap beneath the warm moon.

So next time you spin, let your fabric come loose,
For laughter and stories, there's always a truce.
Woven echoes of joy, inseparable thread,
Leave a trail of fun wherever you're led.

Tales in Textiles

A polka-dot scarf once plotted a caper,
It dreamed of adventures far beyond the paper.
'Let's sneak to the party, we're fashion's delight!'
'Fling your colors, oh friend, under disco lights!'

A button was winking, smirking quite high,
'Tell me, is that truly your best try?'
The line-up of fabrics began to conspire,
'The tale of our escapade, we cannot tire!'

The woolen mittens thought they could dance,
But instead tumbled over, lost in a trance.
'The story is grand, though we came in a bunch,
For nothing beats friendship, and a good wiggle lunch!'

So if you have fabric, find joy in its bend,
Spin stories together, let each thread blend.
In the world of textiles, hilarity reigns,
With laughter and color that brightens the lanes.

The Intriguing Knot

Deep in the drawer, a mystery wrapped tight,
The knot shook and jiggled, much to its delight.
'Why do you stare, when I'm free as a breeze?'
'Let's tango and twirl like the leaves in the trees!'

Two shoelaces giggled, their tips having fun,
'We'll trip up the folks, oh, won't that be fun?'
And the knot winked and twisted, preparing its game,
'Your foolish tomfoolery, I'll surely inflame!'

So they gathered their fabric—all wrinkled and worn,
Planning their antics from the evening till morn.
A merry procession of clips and of strings,
Turning domestic chaos into laughter that rings.

For each fray and each twist carries wit in its core,
In knots and in fabric, there's always much more.
So untie your worries, and spin on the spot,
For life is a giggle, and laughter's the plot.

Ribbons of Time

In a world where socks play tag,
And slippers dance a jig,
Buttons gossip on the line,
A patchwork quilt's a wig.

Dust bunnies hold a meeting,
While curtains sway in cheer,
The clock's hands form conga lines,
In this fabric-filled frontier.

A scarf whispers secrets,
To the buttons on the wall,
As zippers giggle softly,
And yarn begins to sprawl.

So grab a stitch of laughter,
In this playful, quirky rhyme,
For every thread's a chapter,
In the ribbons of our time.

Embroidered Echoes

A needle pricks a storyline,
As threads begin to weave,
The tales of socks and disco shoes,
Dare you to believe?

With every stitch a giggle,
And every button's wink,
The fabric hums a merry tune,
As stitches start to link.

Embroidery on a whimsy,
Each tale a vibrant bloom,
The laughing threads keep teasing,
While spools sway in the room.

What mischief have they sewn today?
What laughter will they bring?
In embroidered echoes,
Life's a nonstop, funny fling.

The Fabric of Dreams

In the quilt of quirky wishes,
Lies a dream that wears a hat,
Buttons play a board game,
With a fluffy, friendly cat.

A tapestry of giggles,
Nestled in the seams,
As a sock sings a melody,
In the fabric of our dreams.

The threads are full of laughter,
Each color, a silly cheer,
As woolly sheep parade about,
Promising fun is near.

So come thread the hidden stories,
In this dreamy, woven play,
Discover all the laughter,
In every stitch we say.

Patterns of Memory

In the patterns of our story,
Lies a quilt of winks and grins,
Where shoelaces tell tales,
Of where the laughter begins.

The patches laugh in colors,
As the seams begin to sway,
With zipper jokes and silly puns,
Inviting us to play.

Each memory a button,
Each thread a tale untold,
In the fabric of our lives,
A treasure chest of gold.

So dance among the stitching,
And twirl among the seams,
For in these woven wonders,
Lies the magic of our dreams.

Chronicles on the Edges

In a drawer where secrets lay,
Lived a sock that lost its way.
It claimed to be a royal pair,
But one was trapped, it had no flair.

The buttons danced upon the shelf,
Mocking shirts that dressed themselves.
They told of nights with wild seams,
And how they stitched up crazy dreams.

A thimble wore a tiny crown,
Laughing at the needle's frown.
"I rule this space with style and grace,
While you poke things, what a disgrace!"

So here within this stitched-up dome,
Lie curious threads that weave a home.
With mismatched bits of fluffy yarn,
They tell of life, both sweet and barn!

Tangles of Forgotten Lore

Once there lived a skein so bright,
It spun its tales both day and night.
Whispers of knitting, tales of thread,
But really, it just wanted bread!

The needles clanked with stories old,
Of cozy scarves and tales bold.
Yet one day they got too entwined,
And tangled hopes were left behind.

A wayward yarn, full of winks,
Dreamed of drinks and silly kinks.
"I'm not just wool, I'm fun and zest,
Come dance with me, and you'll be blessed!"

So gather 'round, let's twist and weave,
In this haven, don't you grieve.
For every knot spins laughter clear,
In the tales that we hold dear!

Kaleidoscope of Threads

A patchwork quilt in colors bright,
Each square has something fun and light.
One tells of a cat with shoes,
Who danced around and sang the blues.

Another shares a tale of socks,
Who threw a party with old clocks.
They laughed and spun – oh what a night!
While toast popped up just out of sight.

Then there's a scarf, quite long and grand,
With stories from a far-off land.
It whispers secrets in the breeze,
Of woolly adventures that aim to please.

So toss your worries, share your mirth,
This crafty blend is full of worth.
With every stitch, a giggle grows,
In the world of threads, anything goes!

The Embroidered Journey

A needle set out on a quest,
With threads of colors, it felt blessed.
It pricked its way through fabric wide,
Finding stories on each side.

Buttons joined in, all in a row,
Each with a tale sparked by a glow.
They spoke of shirts that danced with flair,
And lapels that swayed without a care.

"Oh look!" cried twine, "Here's a sketch,
Of fashion blunders we can fetch!"
With stitches tight and laughter loud,
They made a tapestry, so proud.

At every loop, a nod, a wink,
Adventures spun with every clink.
So follow along, join the fun,
In this journey, we are all one!

Twisted Histories

Once a knight lost his last sock,
He searched his kingdom, quite in shock.
The jester wore it on his head,
Declared himself the sock king, it's said.

A dragon hoarded shiny boots,
But swapped them out for clownish hoots.
In battles, laughter ruled the day,
As knights tripped in a comical fray.

The wizard brewed a potion bright,
But turned his beard into a kite.
He soared above the crowd's delight,
Yelling, "I'll be back! Hold tight!"

So history wrote with a twist and turn,
Lessons lost, yet all would learn.
Laughter thrives in strange old tales,
Where heroes falter, and humor prevails.

Threads that Bind

In a town where shoes were laced with yarn,
People tripped until noon, then tried to charm.
Their tangled feet would dance and sway,
While kittens laughed and chased the day.

A tailor stitched a coat so grand,
But mixed up buttons made them stand.
Instead of sleeves, it had a tail,
And folks wondered, "Is that a whale?"

Two friends decided to weave a boat,
But ended up knitting a playful coat.
They sailed away on laughter's breeze,
Catching the wind with giggles and tease.

In threads of joy, they found their way,
Creating memories with humor at play.
Each knot a story, every loop a grin,
Binding their lives, let the fun begin!

Fabricated Dreams

A dreamer drifted on a pillow of cream,
Searching for treasures inside a scheme.
He found a hat that sang and danced,
And thought, "Oh my! I must take a chance!"

In lands of make-believe so bright,
Unicorns wore socks; what a sight!
They pranced and giggled down candy lanes,
With jellybean rain that cheers and sustains.

A painted frog with a top hat grinned,
As it hosted a tea party — everyone pinned!
Sipping tea while telling tales,
Of wizards riding on playful snails.

In dreams we stitch, with laughter supreme,
Creating stories that sparkle and beam.
Fabricating joy, we share the themes,
In a whimsical world, where wonder redeems!

Loops of Life

In circles we danced, round and round,
Chasing our shadows, happiness found.
With each missing sock, a chuckle would spark,
As we laughed at our footless mishaps in the park.

The baker slipped on icing so slick,
Into a cake, doing a backflip quick.
The guests erupted, cheerful and merry,
As he rolled in sprinkles, an icing dairy.

A looped-up cat chased its own tail,
Tumbling 'round like a furry whale.
The neighbors giggled from their front porch,
As life unfolded with joy, a torch.

In loops we find our funny sides,
With mishaps and giggles, our laughter bides.
Embracing the quirks that each day brings,
In the dance of life, we twirl on strange wings.

www.ingramcontent.com/pod-product-compliance
Lightning Source LLC
Chambersburg PA
CBHW060121230426
43661CB00003B/284